# The Oracle of Luna:

## Meditations with the Moon Goddess

by
Bridget Engels

# DEDICATION

This book is dedicated to the Sister's in the
Circle of Luna - Past, Present and Future.

*"Bide by the moon, follow her glow,*

*By the light of the new we renew and grow.*

*By the waxing quarter our determination shows,*

*By the full moon's light our desires we know.*

*By the waning quarter we ebb and flow,*

*By the dark moon's presence we return what we've sown.*

*Bide by the moon, Follow her glow."*

*-Unknown*

Luna was the sacred Goddess in ancient Roman times and she was the divine embodiment of the Moon.

What does Luna mean now?    In a word: *Magick*

Her beams reflect the passage of each season without being completely attached to them like the Sun. Luna's celestial energies create the ebb and flow of the tides not only in bodies of water but in us well.

Healers, Witches, Pagans and Sages since ancient times have honored and learned from the moon for planting and harvesting crops as well as creating calendars.

As women; we are profoundly and intuitively connected to the Moon's energies. Each 28 days she reflects the menstrual cycle from the gradual hormonal buildup to the period and then the release and then the cycle begins again. This is an echo of the three phases the moon:
New Moon – Full Moon – Dark Moon. This cycle is also symbolized in the image of the Triple Goddess and her faces: Maiden - Mother-Crone.

In founding and leading the Circle of Luna here in Seattle, I have energetically linked our moon rites to the powerful Waxing and Waning of the moon.

The Waxing moon is a time to grow and build. It is the period between the New Moon and the Full Moon. The Waning moon is a time to dissipate and lessen. It is the period between the Full Moon and the New Moon.

We are a small but mighty circle of women who chose to gather, celebrate and glow with the Moon Goddess in all her cycles and seasons. With each rite, we tap into the energetics of the moon phases, the Wiccan Sabbats, and the cycles of the seasons as well as honoring and invoking the Lunar Goddess(s). We incorporate chanting, drumming, singing, dancing & movement, poetry, drama, guided visual meditation and celebration with each Esbat. We embody the Goddess as we are all priestesses when we are in circle together.

This book is a sample of some of the guided meditations I have written and led for our Circle of Luna over the past five years. These guided meditations are the heart of our rituals and take us into a Theta brainwave state for accessing and activating healing, creativity and intuition much like the Moon's energy. They can be accompanied with drumming, props, smudging, aromatherapy, candles, etc....

We have found that honoring and being in tune with Luna's powerful and unique energies; we feel our own divine femininity can be explored, creating fulfillment and wholeness within us and to each other. This creates positive waves of vibrational energy which we can then take out into the world in which we live to influence balance and wholeness.

In writing and leading several women, including myself, on a journey in ritual circle with these guided meditations; it is my hope to inspire others to connect to Her cycles, and to the rhythms of the seasons and tap into the divine femininity within all of us.

So take a journey with Luna and celebrate your divine femininity...

# AKNOWLEDGMENTS

I would like to gratefully acknowledge Janice Van Cleve
for her support, mentorship, wisdom and friendship over the years.
Also gratitude to my Moon Sisters: Julie, Brooke, Kathryn for their
active dedication and generosity of energy since the beginnings
of Circle of Luna.

Special thanks to animal companions(doggies): Ruf, Daisy and Buck
for their valuable spiritual assistance.

# CONTENTS

# new moon

Power to grow and make a new direction
Plant the seeds of your intentions
Open up to new possibilities
Maiden aspect

# 1. Rhiannon ● December New Moon

Get comfortable now and take a few deep breaths. In and Out and In and Out. Relax and let go of all your cares and concerns of the day and just go within…. Close your eyes.

Now feel yourself walking in a dark, deep snow-filled forest in a dark winter night.

The air is icy crisp and the sky above the tall fir and cedar trees is deep indigo with stars shining like diamonds above. It is silent in these deep ancient woods and just the sound of your footsteps crunching in the snow is heard. You are walking slowly forward into the deep, snowy woods this night.

You stop at a huge and ancient cedar tree and you look up. The sky is clouded over and the snow begins to fell rapidly. You put your hand on the bark of this tree and you feel a deep hum flowing from the tree into your heart. Now you become melting snow and you sink deeper and deeper into the cold earth. Your energy is transmuted and you feel yourself twisting, turning and shapeshifting through the root structures. Deeper down you go into the place beneath the trees-even more silent – but very alive with the forces of Mother Earth.

Then you push back up onto the surface of the snowy forest once again. This time you are weightless – like air; a glowing translucent, light body and you are hovering just above an icy stream in the dark forest.

You hear a high-pitched singing in the air….. Someone or something is approaching you from the black dense woods.

Emerging from the darkness is a beautiful white horse and a woman riding atop of it with flowing golden hair.

She is wearing a silvery cloak and crystal band headdress with a shimmering white long veil. White birds are hovering above and around her as they are once invisible and now in focus. She has a serene and otherworldly gaze. The ground beneath her and her horse illuminates with a glowing glittery white light as they move toward you. You sense a magical and powerful force around her.

She stops near the icy stream and with an outstretched hand; she quietly motions you to take it.

You are ephemeral and you take her hand and at once are lifted onto the back of her white horse.

Galloping onward into and through the snowy night; you feel as if the white mare and this powerful Lady are not touching the ground anymore.

Faster and more fleeting- you fly forward higher into the snow covered hills and up into the icy mountains. The magical birds are circle around you all and you feel they are lulling you to sleepy trance. Aaaahh…

Transported, you fly higher like the wind up above to the highest peak of the snowy mountain and see that the crescent sliver moon is

rising above in the starry winter sky and there are some Northern Lights glowing on the horizon.

The Lady now disappears and now it is just you and the white mare illuminated and transcendent riding up, up to the top of the snowy crags of the great mountain. You feel completely free and sovereign; without fear and without burdens of earthly existence….Yesssss!

Ascending higher until you are touching the surface of the white, glittering sliver Moon . You are powerfully energized with an unknowable force through your spirit body. Suddenly the luminescent face of the Lady who was riding the white horse with you comes into your mind.

*She speaks to you:*

"I am Rhiannon and I have been carrying you so that you can be transformed wholly with no unhealed part of you affecting your sacred spirit.

Are you ready to take your dreams into the future?? I am the force of the moon and I will help you release past burdens and patterns that no longer serve you. You are complete Magic and Power.

You are now ready to face your future with complete confidence knowing that any dreams you have will now unfold in perfect timing for you. Take heart and trust that your ultimate magnificence is shining forth now!!"

You feel the energizing power of her words shattering your mind and spirit. You feel it and know it to be true for you.

The white mare is beneath you galloping even faster back through the sky now after circling around the moon on a white silvery path of stars. The magical birds sing with their ringing songs. Your life force is being transported back to the mountain top.

Rhiannon is waiting at the top of the peak-glowing in her silvery flowing robes for you. The mare and the magical birds stop. She swoops up and sits on the horse. Gently you are seated with her and together you fly down the side of the snowy, moonlit mountain. Down, Down, Down….. back into the dark forest.

Now in the dark forest; she gently lifts you down off the horse and she disappears through the dark air.

You are standing in front of the huge cedar tree again where you started your journey…You melt as liquid snow again and you flow back down into the cold earth again twisting and transmuting through crowded tree roots and pummeling through rocks and soil until you suddenly come up through the surface of the snow again.

You are whole again in your human form. You have been empowered and changed by the Goddess Rhiannon on this cold, moonlit winter night.

You have moved through other realms and your spirit has ascended to a higher vibration. You are total freedom, creativity and power! Healed and illuminated; you will become your future.

You thank Rhiannon in your heart for her visit and blessings tonight.

Slowly you walk through the snowy night woods until you see a small cabin ahead. As you get closer; you see a fire in the hearth. You approach and then open the door and sit down in the comfortable chair warming your hands in front of the fire….Aaaahh…

Remember your journey with Rhiannon tonight. Feel her gifts she has given you in your core being. Now slowly take a few deep breaths and when you are ready….come back to present time and place.

*YOU* are true Magnificence, Alive, Energized and Empowered to carry your highest dreams forth. Blessed be!

# 2. Brigid ● February New Moon

Take a few deep breaths and close your eyes. Release all your cares and concerns from the day. Get comfortable now. Ground and center and gently go within. Let it all go.

See yourself walking on a ridge. Your white long wool robes flapping in the chilly wind.

The late winter sun is setting over the tops of the highland hills. Here and there snow and ice are scattered from the last storm over the rocks and brush.

You make your way to the top of one of the ridges and notice the steep drop down. A wild wind rips up from behind you and throws your footing off balance. Your arms flail out to try and balance and catch yourself from falling but it is too late.

You are twirling and falling down, down, down the steep dark ravine. After slowwwwlllyyy falling, your body lands on a grassy mound with a thump. The surface is a curved roof top made of solid earth. You try to stand up and dust yourself off but again slip and then slide down the top of the mound and land at what looks like an entrance into a dark tunnel. Afraid and breathless; you gather your courage to enter this dark doorway. Darkness surrounds you outside and it feels like the entrance may lead you to shelter. You enter the doorway into the tunnel of the mound.

Carefully you move forward placing your hands in front of you. It is silent and the only sound is your breath and your slow footsteps. The tunnel now leads to a stairway down that opens to a dark circular cavern. There is no light except for a tiny flame emanating from the middle of the floor. You move closer to the flame and gaze at it for awhile feeling its hypnotic pull.

The flame begins to grow a little higher as you feel entranced. It grows slightly higher and now you see the surface of the ceiling and walls have reddish, deep orange hues. Still staring into the flame- you can now make what looks like a shape of a woman's face contorting with the flame as it grows ever taller and brighter.

A pair of eye flashes out of the flame. You jump back in fear. Suddenly the flame bursts up into a full height of a flame-like woman shape before you. Stepping back from her heat and unearthly force you try and look away but her piercing eyes are locking deep into your soul now keeping you frozen in your place before her.

There are sounds of feet moving soft and steady somewhere near the stone cavern walls now. The footsteps grow closer & closer. Into the cavern come thirteen shrouded and wearing all white priestesses forming a circle silently around the tiny central flame. Humming a low chant they stand facing the flame which appears to be getting higher and larger by the minute. The shadows of the priestesses on the walls of the cavern leap and grow- their shrouded faces are illuminated.

The flame now expands and shoots up into a flaming woman with golden flame-like hair and a green mantle over a white flowing gown. She is radiant and extremely powerful.

She speaks now: "I Brigid, now charge you all to enliven your passions and know that within you is an invincible flame that will always be there to give you courage and inspiration. Prepare Sisters, to reach within me and find where you can heal, grow create and love for yourself in your own lives.

One by one each Sister comes forth and touches Brigid's flame and then cradle a little fire with their cupped hands. They are holding sacred flames that do not burn their hands. Each sister steps back into circle surrounding the Goddess Brigid cradling their sacred flames and their humming turns into a chant:

"Follow the light within…follow the light within…." Over and over as it becomes more powerful and you lose yourself in the intensity. Just then, Brigid fixes her glowing eyes directly onto you…

She speaks into your mind: "What will your flame look like Sister? What special passion do you carry within you that you want to express? Come forth and take from me…cradle this flame. May it kindle your own passion and inspire others to do so when you leave here. Honor this flame and Never let it go out…Let it shield and surround you."

You walk forth to her and reach your hands into her flaming body even though you fear being burned-you are unhurt and the sacred fire you cup into your hands fills your heart with strength and love. You stand in circle now with the other priestesses are all chanting a little quieter now. Soon they begin to move out of the sacred fire chamber up the stairs and so you follow them. You turn back to look at Brigid but she is one and just a tiny flame is lit in the center again.

You follow the other priestesses out of the cavern and into the dark, crisp new moon night. Carrying all the scared flames in their cupped hands still they make their way up to a hilltop with a clearing. You see the circle of large ancient stones as they all gather in within.

They begin to dance slowly intertwining in and out of small circles and linking their arms while still holding their flames in one cupped hand. Gaily smiling and laughing you join this unique and beautiful dance beneath the ancient stones.

Suddenly they stop their dance and begin to one by one walk out of the stone circle in different directions. You walk out too guided by your little flame. You walk into the dark hilltops and snow begins to fall gently.

You now make out the ridge that you walked on that you came from earlier. Gradually a glowing light blazes a pathway before you to the ridge and so trusting that Brigid is guiding you… you follow the lighted path in the dark snowy night.

You step over a ledge and fall gently falling in the air unafraid deep into the void….You land gently onto a snowdrift and breathe deeply. You are safe and feel honored, eternal and inspired. Slowly take a few more breaths and gently let yourself come back to present time and place.

When you are ready; open your eyes…. Thank Brigid for her gifts and your journey with her.

Blessed be…..

# 3. Sacred Snake & Diana ● March New Moon

Get comfortable now. You can lay down on the floor with blankets/pillows or sit upright and take a few deep breaths...close your eyes. Feel yourself begin to relax and go within.

Now slowly dissolve your ego self and look within to your third eye Chakra between your eyebrows. Relax and let go of all your cares and concerns of the day.

Our journey begins with you as a large rattlesnake snake deep in the cold ground between crevices of rock and dirt and coiled up tight. You have been hibernating during the winter months. Nestled in the frozen earth; it feels familiar, safe and dark like a womb.

The first rays of dawn are just peaking over the mountains that you are settled within. You hear the sound of squirrels scratching on the surface of the soil above you. You then begin to feel a slight stirring in the ground around you. The hard soil is shifting around you. It is time to move...

You slowly begin to wiggle and wind out of your coiled up position slowly and with instinctive effort you unravel through the rock and soil. You slither slowly to the surface towards daylight. Your snake eyelids pop open when you reach the fresh mountain air. Your tongue snaps in and out. Aaaahhhhh!!

Breathe it in. You feel the fresh mountain air on your face and see early morning sun rays over the mountain tops. You are above ground once again. You hear chirping of birds in the trees above you.

You writhe through tender Spring shoots as you look for an insect or two to chew on. The air is cool but promises warmth later.

You are aware of insects buzzing in the distance; so you wind your way slowly towards a large meadow with young wildflowers and early grass. Frogs are beginning to echo in the wetlands and a stream is gurgling in front of you now. Gradually, you wind your way into the sounds of life. Buzzing insects, Robins singing, larks and hawks crying out, frogs belch out and now you hear the quiet footsteps of a family of deer taking a drink ahead from the fresh mountain stream. They sense your approaching and wander off. Now you are crossing the stream and move up and over the banks and wiggle your way into the grass.

Your tongue pops out and you sallow a beetle. Then your tongue whips out to snag a small fly. Yesssssss!
It is good to be eating again. You feel some new energy flow into your snake body. The sun is moving overhead in a blue sky and start to feel its warmth. It is a Spring sunshine filled day and you sense the universe is bursting with life. Yesssssss!....

You now come to an opening in the green grass and decide to ask in the sun. Hours pass. Wildlife sounds of movement pass through your hearing. A swallow swoops down and pecks your head startling you. A tentative butterfly flutters daintily around you. "Follow me.." she whispers. "Follow me." You try to move your inner muscles but your skin is staying on the ground. Aaaahhhh…. Feels good to shed your old skin!

Steadily your old skin is cast off to disappear into the earth once again. You now can move forward faster and with ease to chase the butterfly that is dancing in the air above you and eat another innocent fly that happens to be in front of your tongue. Yesssssssss!

You are renewed again and writhe faster up a mound in the center of this meadow. You finally reach the top and stop at this resting place and begin to bask in the warm, late afternoon rays of the sun that feels wonderful on your new skin.

Feel the grass shooting up through your muscles and ligaments and the wildflowers brushing up against your ribcage. Listen to the hum of the insects buzzing in your ears and the message of the butterfly of rebirth and transformation. Hear the birds as they tell you to live, live, live and sing again. Your body, your mind and your entire spirit is alive with the magick of this Spring day in the sunshine. It infuses every cell of your being!

Stay here as the reborn snake on the mound in the Spring meadow until the sun goes down behind the mountains and you hear the sound of crickets in the grass....

A sliver of a New Moon rises in the sky in the East. The Goddess Diana as she speaks to you in your mind now:

"Sister-Just as the snake sheds its old skin to be renewed-so too you will cast off that which no longer serves your spirit. Set your intentions for the Spring season ahead of you. Think of all the seeds you want to plant, nurture and flourish in your own life . And just as the snake sheds its old skin to be renewed- you will also cast off that which no longer serves your spirit. Remember the journey of the snake who now basks on top of the mound in the center of that very alive Spring meadow and honor your own transformation from old to new."

Now take a few deep breaths, wiggle your fingers and toes and when you are ready; come back to present time and place.

Blessed be....

# 4. Your Sacred Animal Guide ● Summer New Moon

*(A slow, quiet drumbeat is nice starting out and a bowl of dried summer herbs/flowers is set beside the firepit outdoors preferably at a beach or forest setting).*

Gather in circle around the firepit and sit down. Get comfortable on a mat or blanket. Close your eyes and go within. Breathe deeply. Let go of all your cares and stresses of the day. We are going on a journey this new moon night…

Now see yourself wandering through a jungle in early evening. It is warm and humid. You are high in the tropical mountains in a dense and active jungle. There are birds squawking, monkeys jumping & climbing on branches above you. The trees are thick with vines. You hear movements of creatures in the brush. Exotic butterflies silently flutter around you. Large insects slowly crawl in the dirt beneath you. All is lush and alive.

You walk towards a clearing on top of the ridge that you have just climbed. You see a ring of stones surrounding a fire pit in front of you. The fire is lit and crackling. Cicadas ring in the evening air and within the tropical trees is a warm, gentle breeze. The sun sinks. Stars slowly emerge in the evening sky.

Suddenly, you feel the earth crumbling beneath you and you are forcefully sucked down a deep hole. It scares you and at the same time all your human senses dissipate. It is a dark, cold, and silent vortex in this hole.

Calm your stunned body and mind and just *BE* in this safe, dark place with no thoughts or human senses now. The place of your spirit….breathe into this place now…
*(Pause for about 3 minutes here)*

Now slowly and ever so gently visualize an animal ally coming into your consciousness. Your deepest self is akin to it. It is a friend and a spirit guide. It can be an owl, mountain lion, wolf, deer, jaguar, dolphin, whale, eagle, Orca, rabbit, wild boar, fox, snake, hawk, butterfly, dog, horse, monkey, dragonfly, tigress, lion, hummingbird, coyote, salmon, buffalo, etc…

Just see what emerges from your inner vision and spirit self…. *(take a few minutes here-about 3 minutes)-stop the drumming here.*

## When you see your sacred animal look into its eyes and ask it:

- Why is it here with you?
- Why did it choose you?
- Find out what your sacred animal guide is teaching you.
- How might you strengthen your bond with it?

**Take a few minutes silently communing with your animal guide in the dark hole deep in the earth.**
*(about 3 minutes)….*

Now thank them for their precious communication with you. After you have conversed with your sacred animal; let it disappear from your inner vision. Now visualize yourself emerge from the dark hole slowly climbing up through space AS your sacred animal…seeing through their eyes… Let your human ego disappear as you become instinctive and wild.

Feel yourself climbing, crawling, swimming, running, lumbering, galloping, pouncing, floating, flying or any combination of those in space now.

Gently with your eyes almost closed, squinting a bit to see somewhat and still in trance state; physically rise as your animal and start to move around your outdoor space…(beach, woods, etc…) Looking out with their inner eyes, without judgement/thought/or expectation. Shapeshifting…still in trance state….moving around however you feel.

*(slow drumbeat starts here if possible)*

Now hear yourself howl, grunt, squawk, chirp, scratch, cry, shout out instinctively as your animal would….

See and feel yourself move a little faster in space….Imagine you are in the jungle again; moving around the firepit at night, very alive with eyes burning with the power and force of your instinctive animal. Feel the wild rhythm and energy of the summer new moon night into every cell of your body, soul and mind.

**(Drumming and animal dancing/movement continues…..picking up pace and energy…)**

When the movement has reached a peak…slowly wind the dance/movements down around the firepit until everyone gradually stops. Open your eyes slowly.

Ground yourself and hold out your arms downward towards the central firepit. Charge your energy into the flames.

## *Say aloud:*

**"As the Phoenix rises from the ashes transformed by flames; Let us be purified that we may be transformed"**

Pass the bowl of dried herbs/flowers and each participant takes a handful and throws into the fire saying:
**"Purify me!"**

# 5. <u>Demeter</u> ● August New Moon

Take a few deep breaths and center yourself. Sit comfortably and close your eyes. Detach from your cares and concerns from the day and gently go within....

Now begin to see yourself in a wide open field on a golden, warm afternoon. You hear the high grass flowing in the wind. Dragonflies zoom around and swallows playfully swoop and fly above you in this late Summer field. The scents of dry grass and blackberries warmed by the late afternoon sun and plums hanging from a nearby plum tree surround you. Cicadas buzz high in the cottonwood trees at the edge of this field.

You could stay here for an eternity basking in this late afternoon peacefulness. But something now beckons you to get up and move on through the high grass that waves slowly in the soft breeze.

You walk towards a slow running creek at the edge of a slow running creek at the edge of the field under the Cottonwood trees. You dip your hands into the cool water and rinse your face. Refreshed, you walk on...Moving forward quietly; you see that the creek dries up just ahead and turns into a wide path. You are walking on this now and it seems to be getting warmer and dustier.

Suddenly, the path dissipates and stops near a vast cornfield. The corn stalks are high, green and vital. The ears of corn are hanging off the stalks, ripe for picking. The sweat is rolling down your face and arms from the heat and so you sit down in front of the cornfield to cool off. The sun is starting to sink in the sky and is casting long, golden beams through the corn stalks. You feel content now; bathing in the warmth and bounty.

You hear a soft rustling sound now coming from within the cornfield. The noise is getting louder as you sense someone or something walking towards you and pushing aside the stalks gently but with steadfast purpose.

Who or what could it be? The sun is a low orangey/reddish sphere hovering over the horizon. A statuesque
figure now appears in front of you…she is draped in flowing golden robes. A garland of sunflowers and wheat crown her head. Two small red hawks perch on each of her shoulders. She cradles a lovely basket of fruit in her arms. You sense her powerful, ancient energy. You stand up to greet her.

"Greetings Sister, I am Demeter. I have walked the ages to ask you this question, my dear child of the Goddess.
What is it that you will harvest in your life this Lughnasa?? Think on this and tell me your thoughts…I will hear you"!

*(Pause for about 3 minutes)*

"I hear your thoughts and I will bless your accomplishments with Abundance and may you now reap the rewards of your hard work. Your heart is true and your spirit is pure. Go now with my blessings of bounty.
Your own harvest will now begin. She hands you a gift from her magick basket. It is a golden pear that shines.

You accept her gift and thank her for it. Swirling around with a supernatural speed; Demeter slips back through the cornfield into the sunset and disappears with her hawks flying above her in the air circling above her. Where Demeter stood there now grows a golden pear tree.

You smile and with a feeling of gratitude; reach up into the sky with its last rays of glorious sunlight. Then you turn around and head back in the direction of the path that brought you here. The stars are coming out and the new moon sliver shines dimly in the night sky.

When you are ready take Demeter's blessing and your vision of what you would like to harvest in your life. And fix your intentions, goals of your life in your mind. They will reap a harvest. If you can think it...it can happen.

Slowly take a few deep breaths and when you are ready ...come back to present time and place. Open your eyes.


Blessed be....

# full moon

Power heightened and flowing
Intentions from new moon nurtured
Intuition and psychic abilities charged
Goals realized and manifested
Mother aspect

# 6. <u>Creiddylad</u> ◯ <u>April Full Moon</u>

Sit down and get comfortable. Quiet your mind and take three deep breaths. Release all your cares and concerns from the day. Close your eyes. Leave all your mundane tasks behind and gently go within.... Relax....

Now see yourself walking through a meadow on a dusky Spring evening. Robins are signing and there are gnats swarming in the air; here and there. The last rays of the sun have set over the horizon from the warm afternoon. The scent of Freesias, tulips, daffodils and wildflowers waft through the air; reminding you that life is fertile now and vitality has returned to Mother Earth. Winter is gone. You leave behind despair, emptiness,
loss and any negative feelings as you walk through this meadow.

A wild rabbit appears out of the brush. It freezes when it sees you. You look into its large black eyes now and get pulled into their hypnotic stare. A part of your consciousness shifts and a new sense of instinct takes over.
You follow the rabbit as it scurries and turns ahead onto a narrowed path that winds through the meadow and into an ancient orchard.

You smell the subtle scent of the white/pink apple blossoms as you walk through this scared and ancient orchard. A few hummingbirds float through the blossoms. You notice the rabbit looking back at you; frozen with its nose twitching and watching you with its black eyes as if it knows a secret. You instinctively move with the rabbit now as it leads you to a beautiful and sacred spring and then disappears.

You stand at the edge of the large, circular spring that is lined with flowers. Aaahhh, how lovely it all is...

You now feel compelled to bathe in the water and take off your clothes and step into the clear, deep pool. It is so refreshing and purifying to swim nude. Floating on your back; you see the rising full moon above you. You are utterly at peace; floating in this healing sacred spring.

You now feel as if someone or something is staring at you and you flounder a bit and then swim towards the being. The moon is shining behind her as you see a gorgeous figure of a woman with a crown of feathers around her head and flowers and vines weaved throughout her long, blonde hair.

She smiles down at you and says:

"Sister... do not fear; I am Creiddylad and I want you to enjoy and honor yourself. I am the Goddess of self-love and moon-flowing love. I am the eternal May Queen. I appear with you when your heart longs for love, healing and bliss. I answered your call...."

She opens her hands and lifts her arms up to the sky and now hundreds of soft flowers and blossom petals float into the sacred spring. They cascade onto you as you relax and float in the deep, cool spring. Your body, mind and spirit are restored perfect peace and you are transformed with Creiddylad's powerful energy flowing through you.

She speaks to you again:

"It is time to return Sister...go now with the blessings of my flowers and this sacred water. Always remember by only truly loving yourself can you love another."

While you are blissfully floating on your back; you envision and feel yourself as the exquisite and eternal May Queen. Your creativity, femininity, unique beauty and inner power have come live and are in harmony with the energies of this moonlit May night. Aaaahhh.

You now swim to the edge of the sacred pool and then step out onto earth. You put on your dry clothes by the light of the powerful and luminous moon and then walk into the ancient orchard and through the moonlit meadow. All is quiet as night has hushed the activity of the day.

You see a lovely bed of Spring flowers and vines that looks comfortable and you lay down to rest upon it.

Closing your eyes now; you are lulled asleep with Creiddylad's blessings, moonbeams, healing sacred spring waters of your own self-love and serenity.

*(take a few minutes and pause here)*

Now slowly, when you are ready…take a few deep breaths. Wiggle your fingers and toes. Come back to present time and place and open your eyes.

Blessed be….

# 7. Erzulie O May Full Moon

Quiet your mind and take three deep breaths. Get comfortable and release all your cares and concerns from the day. Close your eyes. Leave all your mundane tasks behind and gently go within…. Relax….

Now see yourself walking along a tropical white sandy beach. You can feel the warm salty spray of the ocean on your face. The ocean is a bright, turquoise color. The sun is setting low into the horizon after a warm late afternoon. The waves gently roll onto the shore you walk on. You notice many kinds of colorful tropical fish swimming in the water.

Just now, you see a large dolphin swimming towards you near the shore. It looks at you intently and calls out-as if beckoning to you to come closer to her. This female dolphin is a messenger of some sort. She asks you to climb onto her back as she wants to take you somewhere. So you wade out to the waiter and climb onto the dolphin's back.

She starts swimming into the warm tropical water; leaping in and out as you hold onto her through the waves.
You trust this lady dolphin and soon the shore disappears in the distance. The wind and salt spray blow into your hair. The water grows deeper and deeper. You now notice the sun has set in the sky and the evening is setting in. The lady dolphin swims slower now as you come closer to what you make out as a small island.

The full moon is rising and some stars begin to twinkle in the night sky as you and the dolphin swim up to the shore of this island. You are e excited to be somewhere special now even though you do not know where your destination is…As you both pull up onto the shore of this tiny island with palm trees swaying in the humid, warm night air.

You climb of the dolphin's back now and thank her for bringing you here. She makes a whistle/clicking noise and then swims back into the water. The sounds of drum beats in the distance surround the island. The rhythms of the drums are strange and hypnotic. You follow the drum beats to try and see where they are coming from. You walk into the dark jungle with caution and squinting your eyes to see ahead of you.

You now make out a flash of light in the distance and see that there are torches somewhere ahead.
As you walk closer; you see that they are lit in a circle and within this circle of torches is an impressive lady in
a pink long dress dancing in the center to the drumbeats. You approach the lady in the circle closer and can smell the exotic scent of Baobab oil all around her.


The dancing lady in the pink long gown wears a necklace of multicolored shells and feathers around her neck as she swaying and spinning sensually and with something very exotic and foreign about her. You sit down in the sand on the rim of the circle of torches watching her dancing; captivated- she lulls you into a trance….

This hypnotically beautiful lady is African looking with dark black skin and her black hair is piled at top into a stately headdress of pink. You watch her in your trance state swirling faster and faster-spinning to the exotic drumbeats that the drummers outside the circle are beating. They look as if they are also in a trance state.

As you fall deeper into your aware but hypnotic state of mind you have some feelings arise in yourself. You have not felt them for a long time. They are forgotten passions and sensual desires.

Creative visions come forth that have been long buried by the duties of mundane life.

You find yourself standing up and compelled to dance alongside the lady in pink. You begin to twirl and spin alongside her as she now takes your hand and pulls you into her energy field. You see that her eyes are fixed somewhere far off beyond this time and place.

You dance wildly to the frantic drumbeats that fill the warm night air. Swirling, stomping and clapping with abandon; you remember those lost passions and desires and excitement stirs within you…Yeeesssss…!

Laughing and dancing with you the pink lady now looks into your eyes and speaks to you in your mind:

"Sister.. I am the Goddess Erzulie. I am here to help you remember your deepest passions and desires. Do not be afraid of them-honor and obey them as they are your life force……FEEL them now!!"

Soon other women in brightly colored gowns and headdress with necklaces of shells join in the circle and begin to swirl and dance with Erzulie and you. The full moon is rising high in the night sky above this circle of dancing women and Goddess Erzulie leads everyone with a tempo that is yet more intensely powerful. The energy of wild abandon peaks…You scream out….ERZULIE!!!

Erzulie then turns to you laughing and says:

"Sister-haha -you have done well. You have felt those passions within you arise and I am proud of you! Love has returned to your spirit….Take this sacred gift as a reminder to always honor your passions in this life. It is your sacred right and will guide you to be who you are …always. Return to your life and keep your inner fire. You are meant to be inspired and passionate! "

She plucks a beautiful shell from her necklace and hands it to you while she slows her dance down. You take this sacred shell and look at its pinkish essence and feel its energy vibrate in your hand. Then you look up and notice Erzulie has walked into the jungle and vanished into the night.

Now too the other dancing women stop and walk slowly out in different directions into the dark jungle outside the rim of the circle of torches…You are left standing alone in the middle of the circle panting and clutching the sacred shell Erzulie gave you.

Tears of joy and longing begin to trickle down your face as you remember what you sacrificed in life to survive at the expense of your own passions and emotions. They have surfaced this night and charged your spirit and will spark you to live more fully and with passion. You sigh and then turn to walk out of the circle and into the jungle yourself.

Tired and spent you walk towards the sound of waves on the distant shore. You reach the sandy shore and plop down into the warm, soft sand and fall asleep. You feel a kiss on your cheek and open your eyes briefly to see that Erzulie is standing over you smiling and lulling you to sleep. You doze off blissfully still clutching her scared shell. Aaaaaahhhhh…..

Remember your journey this night with Erzulie in the tropical jungle and always honor your inner passions and desires. Now take a few deep breaths and when you are ready return to present time and place. Take your time… Blessed be!

# 8. IxChel ◑ June Full Moon

Take some deep breaths. Ground, center and quiet your mind. Let all your cares and concerns of the day disappear. Surround yourself with white light. Know that this shield protects you in your journey and that you are safe.

One you feel relaxed; listen to the sound of the ocean as the waves break on the shores. In and out...
Tune into your heartbeat. Listen to a rattle pulsing in time with your heart. Feel the rhythm of it.
As you breathe in and out, imagine a white mist forming.

*(a slow beat of a rattle is nice here for about 3-4 minutes)*

Become aware of your feet walking in and out of shimmering, warm white sand now. You hear the ocean
in front of you. You can smell the salt in the air and balmy breeze. Palm trees gently sway against a starry night sky. Above you the full moon is rising.

You walk forward into a jungle up ancient steps lit by small torches. In a clearing, you see a pool of water surrounded by **white stones.** The smell of Sage and Jasmine fills the warm night air.
"You must step into the water to enter my temple" a strong female voice says to you. So, you step into the pool and splash water on your face cleansing your body and spirit. It feels cool on your skin.

When you step out, the mist has cleared completely and you see a small temple in front of you. It is the temple of the Priestesses of IxChel. Torches light the way as you walk slowly towards her throne carved with moving snakes. Seated is a powerful Lady with dark flowing hair and a gold snake headdress, heavy beaded necklaces and piercing eyes. Two Jaguars sit beside her silently gazing at you- protecting her.

She beckons you to come up the steps and be with her.

You slowly step closer to the Lady on the throne. You hear soft chanting of priestesses in the background.

White glowing seashells line her temple walls. She invites you to sit with her. She looks at you and says:

" I am IxChel...You have a question for me?" You tell her *yes*. She smiles at you: "Ask me".

Now ask in *your* mind ... IxChel your questions and then listen well- for she is the great Mayan Goddess

of healing and the Moon and she knows all...

You ask her your questions. She listens to you and then hands you a small silver mirror glowing with moonlight: "Gaze and be transformed".

You look into the sacred mirror and visualize all the changes and growth in your life as it mirrors your highest self. After awhile, you hand back the mirror to the Goddess IxChel. She smiles at you and asks you to hold out your hand as she has a gift for you. She puts a sacred white glowing shell into your hand.

The sacred shell comes from the Sea of Cozumel around the Isle of Mujeras. You thank her for her precious gift. Pour your energy and intentions into this small but powerful shell. You can carry this shell as a reminder of your time with IxChel in her temple.

You now bow to her and then bid her farewell. Slowly and with a heightened sense of awareness you begin to descend the stairs of the temple. You walk past the sacred pool and back into the jungle.

Let the sound of the ocean be your guide and carry you out into the mist-almost floating....

Now when you are ready...take a few deep breaths in and out. Become aware of your feet on the ground, wiggle your fingers and then come back to present time and place....Open your eyes.

Know in your heart that you can always call upon IxChel for healing, creativity, wisdom, power and abundance. She loves you and she will inspire you to powerfully co-create yourself and your world.

Blessed be!

# 9. Abuntantia ◯ August Full Moon

Close your eyes….get comfortable and take a few deep breaths. Forget all your cares and concerns from the day…. Relax….

Now visualize a field in the country on a hot August afternoon. The sky is hazy blue and the field is golden with wheat. The cicadas are buzzing and humming in the distance. You see people in the field reaping the wheat they planted in the Spring with scathes from the old days….they are laboring to get the harvest in by Lughnasa night before the first harvest celebration… You now are one of these laboring people in the field…

You feel your arms and shoulders getting tired from the constant swinging motion and bundling of the wheat.

And the sweat is now trickling down your temples and forehead which you wipe away with your hands.

You take a moments break from your toiling and squinting, look up to see a circle of hawks above in the sky.

They circle ever higher, soaring towards the powerful golden sun.

You close your eyes and feel suddenly different in your body as your arms twist and turn and radically shapeshifting. Terrified but excited you are becoming one with the hawks and feel charged and electrified by the sun's heat and the force of the sun pulls you upwards .

Now you sail with your long wings up and up higher and higher faster towards the golden all powerful orb in the sky. Aaaahhh! Wonderful feeling of flying high in the air and rising above the toiling and heat!

You are flying on the hot air currents and the heat and magical force pulls you sooo close to the orb and its force is magically pulling you to it. You almost get singed you are so close to the sizzling, molten hot surface of the fiery orange glowing sphere and right when you fly as if you are going to clash and burn your feathers –a force stops you mid-air. The voice of the God Lugh speaks to you in your mind:

*"Do not die in my powerful energy my friend-go back now and harness and respect my solar magic for your life on earth is now calling you…"*

Your feathered body dives back with a force speeding back down, down shooting in the air towards the field where you started from. Finally you spread your wings wide to gently lower. You see a shimmering golden light swirling towards the edge of the field close to the forest. You are intrigued and pulled by the force of it closer and lower….. When you get closer you can make out a golden woman-ageless, with yellow/orange flowing robes and shimmering coins trailing behind her long robes. She is waiting for you and lifts her arm out for you to land on it. Floundering you fly wings outstretch to land on her golden flowing arm. Aaaah….you land and perch.


She meets your gaze…a familiar and loving.

*"I am Abuntantia…rest from your toil and look beyond into the infinite abundance that is your destiny…."*

Suddenly you see movement from the forest towards you with your hawk eyes…Someone or something is coming towards you. Quiet and alert you are still perched on the Goddess's arm looking to see what's ahead…

Now one by one…you recognize a being that was from your past or present in your human life on this physical plane and beyond. You instinctively know that they have blessed or taught you in some deep way.

You can see people, beloved pets, friends, lovers, family, aquaintances, teachers, partners, spirit entities, soooo many…they all come towards you silently. There auras are filled with a presence of where and the time in life you were with them. All blessings to you….

You look at them and communicate with them through your soul and thank them. You also get a glimpse of people and places you have yet to know that are further in the distance…Greet and thank them too.

The beings now begin to retreat back into the forest where they came…

Abuntantia's arm is now slowly lifting up and shakes you off her perch. Smiling and loving you she free's you back into the air. The sun is sinking on the horizon and the cicadas are slowly humming…It is peaceful in the August twilight as you fly in the air circling happily with a feeling of deep gratitude and peace.

Twinkling stars now appear the bright majestic moon is rising in the summer's night sky. You fly softly towards the moon in the warm night sky and feel the powerful pull.

Then flapping, twisting, and shapeshifting again your human body comes back to form….

Come back to the present place and time…..Slowly and gently take a few deep breaths and recover …

Remember your gratitude to Abuntantia for showing all the beings that have blessed you in this life and your journey.

Be grateful for their gifts and the gifts of the earth mother who supports you on your journey.

Honor the harvest of what you have sown, worked and now begin to reap this moment… You can now gently open your eyes.


Blessed be!

# 10. <u>Triple Goddess</u> ☾ <u>September Full Moon</u>

Take a seat in circle or on your own and get comfortable now. You can lay down on the floor with blankets/pillows or sit upright and take a few deep breaths…close your eyes. Let go of all your cares and concerns of the day. Feel yourself begin to relax and go within. You are going on a journey….

Now imagine yourself on a dark, early autumn night at the edge of a lake. There is a slight chill to the air.
The waves lap up onto the shore near your feet. The full moon is rising over the horizon white and shimmering; shining a path on the surface of the water to you. A small wood boat floats near the shore; waiting for you there. You walk into the water and get in the boat and then push off with the paddle into the lake.

You paddle into the moonlit path on the surface of the water further towards the middle of the lake. You are feeling the mysterious pull forward. You keep paddling towards the other side of the lake.

There is an inlet ahead of you; partly obscured by trees. You softly paddle into the dark and silent inlet. It is now leading you into what looks like the mouth of a river. Your boat lurches forward as the current beneath you beneath you becomes stronger and swifter. It makes a turn and then another and twists more and more.

Large rocks jut out from the sides of the river as you instinctively, float through them all avoiding all danger.
As you paddle through these rapids; you look up to see in the darkness what looks like cliffs forming an arc.

As your boat passes under the cliffs you can now smell salt water on the breeze.

The current pulls you forward faster now into a choppy, vast sea. The moonlight seems to have vanished with clouds covering the sky. You suddenly feel lost, alone and afraid in this sea. What's worse is that there is a funneling whirlpool and it's sucking you down into it!

You scream out for help. Aaaaahhhhh! Just as your boat is careening on its side into the voracious whirlpool- you sense a force of power and strength surrounding you. A high pitched hum of a woman's voice sings high on the air. Suddenly the whirlpool ceases and your boat regains its balance on the sea. A strong breeze pulls you forward and you lose consciousness from your fear and exhaustion.

You are pulled through the stormy sea and finally onto a shore. You blink awake and notice this brilliant white shore illuminated by the moonlight. Little round, white stones glow from the moonlight that is shining in a clear and starry sky above you. What an utterly serene and lovely place this is and utterly silent. Your soul is at peace. You get up and walk out of your boat and onto this shore of glowing white stones.

You now sense some movement of energy coming towards you and hear the same high-pitched hum in the air when you were in the whirlpool on the stormy sea.

Appearing before you now is an ethereal woman. Tall, radiant, ancient and powerful as her force emanates all around her. Gravity pulls you closer to her. Her silvery gown and white flowing hair seem electrified with lunar energy. Her face is three in one that is constantly turning and changing. It is hard to distinguish her features. Full and white, half black shadowed and white, all black shadowed and now changing to white again.

She speaks to you in her otherworldly voice:

" I am Luna. I have been with you and the Earth since the beginning and I will be there at the end of time. I show myself to you in all my guises as I sail through the heavens and your life in all the seasons…your seasons. I empower, I illuminate, and I transform life. Wherever you are; you will have my eternal guidance while you walk this Earth.

Think back daughter, to the moment when you were a teenage girl. Your eyes wide open and innocent, with youthful energy. What were your thoughts, dreams and motivations at that time? Do you remember your youthful power?

Now think back again when you were a 30 year old woman… remember who you were around or with in relationship and in work or school. How did you express your power and energies? Savor the life force of those years their fertileness.

Now think ahead when you will be a 65-70 year old woman. How will you best use your wisdom, power and energies?

I am and you are all three cycles of life-ever intertwining, ever transforming and ever giving. Throughout all the endless cycles of life, death, rebirth- Maiden-Mother-Crone ….

Take this gift as a reminder of your journey this night and my blessings to you…

I will always shine my light into your spirit no matter what cycle of life you are in. Go now and rest".

*(She places a white small moon stone in your open palm now while your eyes are still closed…)*

She points with her glowing outstretched arm towards a white washed cottage tucked above the embankment.

You bow to Luna and slowly turn and walk towards the cottage. Turning around, you see that she is gone but the moon in the sky has become so enormously full and radiant- it shines a glittering light all around the lake You are tingling and charged with lunar energy and feel empowered, healed and peaceful.

You now get to the door of the cottage and open it and walk inside. There is a warm fire and a soft bed against the wall. You lay down and rest awhile… (pause her a few minutes)

Now slowly take a few deep breaths in and out. Wiggle your fingers and toes. When you are ready come back to present time and place. Open your eyes…

Blessed be!

# 11. Cave of Goddesses ○ October Full Moon

Take a few deep breaths and center yourself. Sit comfortably. Quiet your mind and close your eyes. Detach from your cares and concerns from the day and gently go within….We are going on a journey…

Now picture yourself walking through a high rocky and mountainous trail in the late afternoon. It is starting to get a bit chilly and you pull your shawl over your head and shoulders. Walking one step in front of the other; you feel a pull towards an outcrop of rocks ahead.

You now arrive at an opening in the face of a mountain. There is a dull, golden light emanating from within; so you enter. It is a deep cavern that is silent except for your breath and the dripping sounds of moisture from the cave walls to the ground. You press on towards the dim light ahead.

Walking forward on the slippery stones and turning a corner you stop in amazement. The surface of the walls are covered with ancient mineral drawings and carvings of what look like bison, horses, birds and outlines of human hands. You make out a few primitive human figures. They are very surreal in the dim light. You also notice how these drawings made of ochre, burnt sepia, rust, black and white are painted on top of bulging rock surfaces —so they create organic forms. They seem petrified yet in motion too. You move ahead with the big curve in the cavern that show a mass of galloping horses and eventually an upside down "V" shaped outcrop of a rock.

Staring right back at you is an immense and powerfully charged drawing in mineral paint of a wide-hipped, amply breasted woman who is holding a crescent shape in her left hand. Ancient and enduring; she looks like she has been presiding over this sacred chamber for thousands of years.

The flickering, warm light source is getting a bit stronger as they make the animal cave drawings an ancient woman look animated.

You can make out a low humming sound. So you follow the humming down into a lower circular level of the cave. Ahead you can see a group of nine large, upright standing stones. Each stone is about ten feet high and in the center of this stone circle is a flaming firepit. You sense something is about to shift now as you walk into the center. There is a surge of powerful energy in the atmosphere around you.

The stones look like they are moving! You stare at them in awe. It is as if something is trying to break free from within each stone. The stones now begin to shake. Then some magical force bursts each of the stones. You look on unbelievingly as they have transformed into ancient women whose larger than life forms have faces. You look into their painted faces now and see the power of real Goddesses that are alive!

They wear flowing robes, headdresses and jewelry of a far off time but their faces look familiar to you.

*(start a slow drumbeat here for about 3 minutes…)*

Isis, Kali, Danu, Freya, Brigid, Diana, Hecate, Astarte, Gaia…..link arms and start a circular dance. Soon they are whirling fast around you; gathering speed and creating wind and energy. Hear their powerful voices lifting and echoing from the ground to the ceiling and all around the cave forcefully now. The fire flames leap up and dance across the cave walls.

What you see now astounds you even more. It looks like *your face* as a young woman, you also see your mother, your grandmother, her mother, your aunts, your sisters and several generations of maternal ancestors.

YOUR history is part of this cave now; etched in the stone of this sacred cavern which is imbedded within mother earth.
*(drumbeat stops now...)*

Just now, the dancing nine Goddesses; slow to a stop back into their original places in the circle you first saw them in. The flames of the firepit have died down to embers. But you are glowing with a pulsating force and magickal Goddess energy is coursing through your veins into every cell of your body. You are awakened, divine and very alive!

Take a moment to remember this feeling. Now speak their Goddess names out loud and your maternal ancestors names that you know out loud in this cave. Honor them. Thank them for their life force and creation energy within you. The nine standing circle of stones are peaceful and the cavern is silent except for the dripping sounds of moisture.

Slowly...you turn to head back towards the cave entrance. You are still in a trance state but you try and regain your consciousness with each step you take. You leave the cave and walk out into the fresh free air of the night outside. Above you, Luna shines her magnificent full moon beams onto the rocks, trees and lighting your path ahead. You walk in her luminous white light on this path away from the mountain cave and into the trees.

Now slowly and gently, take a few deep breaths. Wiggle your fingers and toes and when ready....come back to present time and place.

Acknowledge your journey and know that whenever you need courage, perspective, and strength; you can return to the sacred cave of the Goddesses for support and to remind you that you are part of the eternal cycle of life and that she is always within you.

Blessed be...

# dark moon

Completion of the cycle - the ebb
Releasing and banishing energy
Secrets and mysteries
Silence, stillness, death before new life
Crone aspect

# 12. <u>Hecate</u> • <u>September Dark Moon</u>

Sit down and close your eyes. Ground your energy and take a few
deep breaths. See yourself in the room you are in.
Be aware of the walls around you, the floor below you and the ceiling
above you. As you see yourself in the room, see a white mist start to
fill the room; rolling in and becoming more and more dense all
around you. You are surrounded by this thick white mist now....

Now the mist starts to disperse and fade away; leaving you standing
on a rocky mountainous perch in front of a cave. On either side of
the cave are lit torches. You enter the cave and walk downwards as it
leads you down into a tunnel. Your journey into the Underworld
begins here....

You keep walking until you hear the sound of running water ahead.
The tunnel now opens into a mighty cavern with a wide, dark river
running through it. You walk to the bank of the river and see
something move toward you through the mist.

A figure in white standing at the bow of a boat appears before you;
hooded and faceless. This boat stops at the bank where you stand.
The hooded figure extends its hand and motions you to embark. You
step into the boat and sit down. The boat gradually departs across the
water and takes you further away from the bank.

The hooded figure silently punts the boat through the misty water.
You glance down and see spectral figures floating in the water. You
know that these are the souls of those who were too afraid to take
the boat ride and then drown in the river.

As the boat stops; the hooded figure motions you to disembark. In
front of you is another tunnel. You look back and the boat has sailed

backwards into the misty river. You now walk tentatively into this tunnel which soon opens into another cavern. The ceiling is so high in this cavern that you cannot see it. The walls are a myriad of different colored crystals. In the center stands a white marble stone altar on which a flame burns; reflecting light onto the walls of the cavern.

You approach the altar but as you come closer to it –it disappears and is replaced by a figure cloaked in black and smelling of Sage and carrying a torch in its ancient hand. Its face is hidden in the dark hood of the cloak but you notice dark gray hair and a headband of stars and moons glimmering around its head. The cloaked figure wears a girdle with a ring of keys hanging around its robed waist.

Amongst the crystals; you see an antiquated large mirror embedded in the wall. The figure raises its arm that holds the torch and motions to this mirror and speaks:

" Traveler…I am Hecate. This is a mirror of visions. You may look into it and see your past, present, future and other lifetimes. It is up to you to work your will on the mirror and see what secrets it will divulge."

*(pause a few minutes here)*

You stand for sometime gazing into the mirror and seeing visions and calling up images you need to see. You can see your child face, your teenage girl face, your adult woman face and finally your older woman Crone face.

After awhile; Hecate speaks to you again and tells you that she has a special gift for you. You hold out your hand and see that it is a card that has a visual message for you. You thank Hecate for her gift and wish that you had something to give to her. She smiles as if she knows your predicament and says:

"The best gift you can give to me is to continue your spiritual journey on whatever path is truest to you. You must vibrate a higher energy and radiate magick in your actions and help make the world in which you live a better place through your deeds."

Pledging to do so; you thank Hecate and with a backward glance at her-you walk towards the cavern entrance carrying the card she gave you in your hand. You walk down the stoney tunnel lit by torches and back to the bank of the river.

The hooded white ferryman waits for you on the boat that will take you back across the mystical river again. You have returned and disembark and thank him for his service. You walk back up the steeply sloped tunnel. Soon you are standing once again at the opening of the cave where you started your journey.

Visualize the magickal card that Hecate gave you. What image comes to mind? What message does it have for you?

You notice a white mist rolling in; becoming more and more dense. It surrounds you and obscures everything. The mist begins to break up now and as it does so; take a few deep breaths. When you are ready come back to present time and place. Look at the walls around you, the ceiling above you and the floor below you.

You have returned from your journey with Hecate in the Underworld. Remember what you saw in the mirror in her crystal cavern and her gift to you. Honor her divine wisdom and remember to uphold your pledge to continue your spiritual journey heighten your vibration to help the world in which you presently live.

Blessed be....

# 13. Morrigan ● October Dark Moon

Get comfortable and release all your cares and concerns from the day. Hood your cloak now covering your head. Deep breath in and out. Feet resting on the floor. Gently go within....we are going on a dark moon journey....

Now see yourself walking beside a boggy marsh on a dark moon October night. There are sounds of bullfrogs echoing in the distance. A mist hovers above the water. There is a chill breeze in the air that creaks through the bare branches in the woods that skirts the edge of this marsh.

You silently walk on the pathway around the water as it leads you into an unknown forest. Your feet crunch quietly on the frosty fallen leaves covering the earth. The trees in these woods are ancient and powerful as their branches twist outwards and upwards like giant, wicked fingers. Here and there you hear the lonely hoot of an owl.

You smell a slight scent of wood smoke in the air and decide to follow it. As you are walking towards this smokey scent; you feel as if someone is watching you sending a chill down the back of your neck. You strain your eyes into the dense woods but cannot see anyone; only the movement of the bare branches in the chilly wind.

You are walking closer to the smoke now. Off in the distance beneath an ancient and magnificent oak tree; you see a small fire crackling with a cauldron hanging above it.

You smell the strong scent of Mugwort brewing from the cauldron. You walk closer to the fire and simmering cauldron with curiosity and some trepidation.

Suddenly, you see a black flash of a raven taking flight and then a figure moving stealthily from behind the oak tree in front of the fire. In a blink of an eye it has vanished. You hear flapping of wings just above your head and you notice a raven is flying just above you from side to side as if taunting you. You walk faster towards the fire and brewing cauldron. The raven disappears and then you see her.

A tall and impressive woman shrouded in dark hood and robes with pale white skin and jet black long hair. She wears a silver sword tucked into her belt of bones. Her secretive dark eyes beckon you forward as she dips a ladle into the cauldron murmuring something foreign and holds a silver cup of hot liquid out to you. You come towards her and accept her drink in your hands. After taking a few sips you realize it tastes unfamiliar.

She now speaks to you:
"You have traveled far Sister. Who are you? What is it that you seek from me on this Dark Moon night"?
You answer her with your name in humility.

She removes her black hood and you see that her face now changes from ancient hag to young and beautiful maiden again repeatedly as she scrutinizes your face. She speaks gain with raw power and a richness that reverberates in the woods.

"I am Morrigan. In legends I have been called Morgan Le Fay and Morgaine; Goddess, Sorceress, Wisewoman, Warrior Queen and High Preistess of Avalon. Like a raven in battle, I conquer any enemy or fear and use my Dark Moon magic to banish the unuseful, the negative and to transform life!! I charge you to follow me and listen to my secret."

A few moments pass and you suddenly feel dizzy and disoriented. Morrigan has vanished and the fire fames grow brighter and stronger. Its firelight casts an orangey glow onto the ancient oak tree that now shows a triple spiral carved into its trunk- ever swirling.

Your legs feel weak and give out under you. Your back is cracking and twisting. You try to scream but all that comes out is a croak. Your arms break painfully as wings shoot out from your sides! You have powerful night vision. The unseen becomes seen with your raven eyes.

You see the raven dancing on the cauldron with glowing greenish eyes and it now takes flight. You realize that you have become a raven and now take flight and follow whom you now know to be Morrigan the Raven. Your bird heart beats to the rhythm of the universe. Seeing the vast forest below you and the mist surrounding the marsh. Above you are distant stars , planets, suns, and galaxies as they move in a spiral forming a universal maze.

Hidden somewhere in that maze is the Dark Moon. Slowly you follow Morrigan and spiral around and around into the turning starry maze high in the sky. You are now inside the center of the turning maze on the dark side of the moon. It is a time out of time where all light and life are sucked out into that cauldron of darkness- the cauldron of Morrigan. In her vast womb, energy and light are gathered until She explodes, radiating birth and new life into the void. The Mother of All and Weaver of the Great Web; she has through eons poured out the contents of her cauldron only to gather it once again, in an unending pattern of birth, death and rebirth.

Suddenly you fly out of the dark cauldron of Morrigan and fly down, down, down till you reach the surface of the misty marsh and feel yourself plunging into the cold water and jumping up again to catch some air.

You see Morrigan the raven circling above you looking down at you from above the water her now transforming into the face of the ancient Goddess and then beautiful Maiden again. You surrender to her magick until once again you feel yourself shapeshifting into your human body.

Gurgling and twisting in the cold, boggy water you gasp for air and swim out onto the shore panting as you pull up onto the sandy dirt. You lay down and feel your human arms and touch your face. Aaaahhhh...you feel safe and exhausted but powerfully charged. Something magical has taken place for you on a deep level.

The sky is lightening in the East. Morrigan is gone. Next to you in the sand is shining black raven's feather. A gift and reminder of your journey to the Dark Moon with Morrigan. Know that you are part of the infinite cycle of life, death and rebirth. You thank her for her gift and journey into her cauldron of transformation this night.

The mist creeps up around you and encircles you like a blanket. Take a few deep breaths and when you are ready; slowly come back to present time and place. Open your eyes. Know that you have been healed and charged. Magic is indeed afoot....Blessed be!

*(This mediation can be enhanced with participants sitting around a simmering pot or cauldron of Mugwort. A slow drumbeat is nice too).*

Blessed be!

# 14. <u>Nephthys</u> ● <u>November Dark Moon</u>

Get comfortable and release all your cares and concerns from the day. Hood your cloak over your head. Deep breath in and out. Feet resting on the floor. Close your eyes and gently go within….we are going on a dark moon journey….

Now…Feel your feet walking in sand. You are in a desert and the vast expanse of the horizon is glowing with a reddish, orangey sundown. It is exquisitely quiet now except for the sound of your feet stepping in and out of the sand.

You are pulled forward by a force towards an Egyptian temple. Two large pillars of a winged woman are at the front entrance of this temple. Their gaze is fixed ahead into the sky. You enter slowly with trepidation into the narrow corridor within. Beyond the first narrow corridor there are steps that lead downwards. Oil lamps are lit on either side of the steps. It is silent and cool inside this mysterious temple but you feel pulled forward by a force. Your heart is pounding and it is the only sound you hear now….

After the last stone step; you enter deep, dark circular chamber. There are hieroglyphs on the walls as well as images of women with outstretched wings and enigmatic symbols that flicker with the oil lamps here and there. There is a stone platform in the center. You stop in awe.

Against the far circular wall ahead sits a woman cloaked in black and gold silently sitting on a carved throne. Her eyes are closed in deep trance…

You step cautiously a little closer to her; afraid yet curious. Then, suddenly, her eyes open. A pair of faraway piercing pair of dark eyes fixed directly on you.

"I am Nephthys. The Lady of the Limit. At the edge of what is and what lies beyond your death…You seek me out, yet you are not ready to crossover??"

*(a slight whisper in the background says three times: "Wings of Nephthys …cover and protect me.")*

You become aware of yourself rising slowly in the air, hovering off the ground. You see your physical body laying on the stone platform beneath you. The Lady is anointing your flat body with some fragrant oils from
an alabaster jar. Incense wafts in the chamber smelling of Myrrh and Frankincense. She does not look up at you hovering above your physical body.

Shapeshifting-you have wings of a large hawk now and with outstretched wings; you flap and rise higher above.

There is no roof in this temple. The ancient pillars open up to the indigo sky. It is a sultry, balsamic moon night.
You are now pure freedom flying round and round, circling the top of the temple up high into the sky towards twinkling stars. Your inner vision is extra sharp. All your earthly suffering has ceased. You are fearless and omnipotent. You are at the edge of what is and what is unknown.

You become aware of a low chanting sound deep within the walls of the temple. It beckons you to return now. Slowly spiraling downward with hawk precision you descend toward 9 priestesses that are shrouded in white. They are chanting around your dead physical body laying there on the stone platform in an ancient language with secret words....

Nephthys moves to the top of the platform nearest your head and stands with arms outstretched. Looking up she says: "Once you go forward into crossing over...you cannot return. Make your choice now!"

Your hawk body lands onto the ground of the chamber and shapeshifts into your human physical body.
Aaaahhh... you are at home within the bones and flesh of your own skin once again. Your spirit and mind feel refreshed; knowing the wisdom of the secret of death, the limitless night sky and kissing the distant stars with your wings.

You slowly awaken out of your deep state of unconsciousness and notice that there is no one in the circular chamber except yourself now. Laying there in your white tunic and headdress; you are regenerated and you slowly sit up and climb off the stone platform and stand up.

You make your way silently but steadily up the stone stairs and out into the upper corridor and then out the entrance of the temple. It is dawn outside. Birds flit above the temple opening. A hawk silently circles high in the air above you. It is slightly chilly. The primordial desert stretches before you and the sun is just peaking over the pyramids.

Slowly, you walk in the sand into the daylight toward some sphinx statues; you take a seat beneath them on a stone bench.

Taking a moment to honor your journey into the Underworld chamber with Nephthys and acknowledging those that have passed on and crossed over this past year in your life. Knowing too that you shall also make this sacred journey sometime and that Nephthys will be there to guide you with her eternal wisdom and magick.

Now slowly take a few deep breaths and come back to present time and place. When you are ready —open your eyes…

Blessed be!

# 15. Kali ● December Dark Moon

Get comfortable now and take a few deep breaths. Close your eyes. Release all the cares and concerns from your day. Ground and center yourself and go within.

Now see yourself walking on a dirt path. It is very cold and the darkness of night is setting in. There are many huge glacial boulders on either side of this path. You are walking towards high snow covered mountains at the edge of this valley. There is no moon in the sky – it is a Dark Moon night.

There is an uneasy stillness hanging in the air as if in expectation of something to come. You continue walk slowly down the rocky dirt path. Suddenly, you hear a loud crashing sound in the distance and look up to see a reddish/orange eruption spewing from one of the mountain peaks into the sky. An avalanche of mud and molten hot lava races down the side of the mountain destroying everything in its path. Trees and bushes are instantly scorched and topple over from its furious path.

You clinch in terror as the molten avalanche is coming your way! You start running into the woods and scurry up the closest and highest boulder you can find. Just in time as the lava is streaming and swirling fiercely in pools around the rock you have just climbed up. Panting you look below and see that the swirling fiery lava is surrounding your rock and is rising higher and higher. The sulfur – like fumes are unbearable.

You start to panic and cry. With tears running down your face and sitting there you hug your knees in despair rocking yourself back and forth. Fear and Doom overtake your very essence! As if the violent volcano eruption was not enough- a wild wind now picks up fanning the lava into fires. No moment in your life has ever been this bleak. With your head down between your knees and rocking back and forth; not knowing what to do you try and raise your head to look up but pass out from the extreme fumes and shock of it all.

After a few minutes of unconsciousness; you sense a dark figure whirling towards you in your mind's eye.

What is this?? It's getting closer and closer to you. Now it's hovering about a foot from your face. It is a dark woman in swirling black cloaks riding a tiger of fire. Her tongue is sticking out and she wears a belt of the cosmos around her waist. A greenish-pinkish light emanates out of the tattood palms of her hands. Her wavy, raven black hair blows in the wind and she stares at you with piercing black eyes. Between her eyes is a third eye of fire. Hovering in front of you she is serene yet powerfully fierce!

Looking deep into your soul you hear her say to you in your mind:

"Even in destruction and darkness, Sister, life is forming renewal for you. I am Kali and I have come to aid you in rebirthing your reality. After all the crisis and death comes a resurrection – always...
Look into the flame between my eyes and you will see new life soon..."

Shaking in dread you see yourself looking at the flame in the middle of her forehead or third eye.

It is not long before you are awakened by the falling of hail around you. Big pellets of hail fall harder and harder. Looking around you see that Kali is gone now. Fully conscious now, you also notice that the vicious lava has started to cool and harden. Steam is rising off the surface. You are drenched and thoroughly exhausted but after awhile you see that there is a subtle lightening in the air around you. You decide that it is time to try and walk on the hardened lava beneath you.

You stumble down off the high rock and put your foot down gently on the surface of the hardened lava. It is solid now. With trepidation, you walk away from the rock and move forward until you can see more light in the sky. It is early dawn now. You sense a presence in front of you walking up in the distance. It is Kali again this time without her fire tiger. You follow her as she leads you up to the plateau atop a rocky hill. Catching up to her; you have reached the top of the plateau and looking out before you is a valley with the first rays of the sun filling it. It's a verdant and green valley below you and looking around you see that Kali has disappeared.

The sun is revealing itself in the sky. A few hawks circle above you. Breathing in the fresh, clean air; you know that you have overcome your struggle and pain to a new day. You thank Kali for guiding and protecting you through the dark night of your soul.

Looking out now to the expanse of the green, living valley in front of you beneath the plateau you realize your own strength. You confidently step into your light and walk down into the valley that is alive with the morning sun.

Refreshed and renewed- take a few deep breaths and when you are ready; slowly come back to present time and place. Thank Kali for her magic and gifts on your journey and thank yourself.


Blessed be!

# 16. <u>Cailleach</u> ● January Dark Moon

Turn off as many lights as you can. Light a candle and take a few deep breaths in and out. Feet resting on the floor or you can lay down. Relax. Close your eyes and gently go within....we are going on a dark moon journey....

Now...visualize the room you are in with your mind's eye. See a thick white mist roll into the room watching it envelope you completely. Surrender to the mist and remove any thoughts or cares from your day......

*(pause for a few minutes here)*

Now the mist dissipates and squinting; you make out where you are. Surrounding you is a massive ring
of stones that is perched high on a cliff. You hear sounds of the sea crashing on the shore beneath you.
A cold, gray sky hovers above this high sea cliff and the ring of stones stand as sentinels overlooking this stormy sea coast.

You notice that there are triple spirals etched into the surface of these stones and you can feel their power. You are seated in the center with your hands placed on the green, heard ground; feeling the force of the undercurrent energy beneath you flowing....

An icy strong wind chills to the bone. You look up and overhead is a strange black cloud moving toward you. Hunching over you grab your knees with fear. Something dark looms over your head and soon you are swept up into this dark cloud; moving through the cold winter sky over the ring of stones and high above the sea cliffs.

The dark cloud surrounds you and pulls you closer. You look up and you see a black long cloak of an ancient woman with wild gray hair pulling you through the sky. You lose consciousness now….There is only the sound of icy sleet pelting against her cloak through the gloomy evening sky.

*(pause for a minute here)*

Your eyelids flutter open and you make out a fire flickering within some kind of ritualistic chamber. A vast slab of stone covers this large cavernous chamber. There are two other passageways leading off into the unknown. Utterly alone; you try to warm yourself beside the fire on the cold ground.

There are skulls and bones of birds and small animals strewn about the floor. This vast burial cairn gives you the shivers. You look up and notice something begin to shift on the surface of a stone wall in front of you.

You see a massive image of an eye looking back at you from the wall. A chill runs down your spine as you hear whispers echoing around you and getting closer; surrounding throughout this chamber.

It sounds like: "Mother of darkness…Mother of light….Earth beneath us; Souls in flight…."

The eye on the wall begins to enlarge and become more illuminated. The whispering ceases and an ancient voice coming from behind the great eye speaks:

"Sister-Why do you come to my sanctuary?

Are you ready to let go of the story of who you thought you were?

Are you ready to resurrect?"

I am Cailleach; Goddess of Death and Transformation and this is my sacred chamber. I am the force that connects all death and transforms it to life again. I am the Keeper of all seeds from the harvest and the Guardian of souls; so that they may return to new life when Brigid comes with her promise of Spring. Stay here until you feel you are ready to Rebirth...."

You feel Cailleach's omnipotent power and it fills your mind and spirit. What you thought was painful, negative, lost or even dead is losing its hold on you.

Cailleach's chanting voice can be heard echoing all around the chamber:

" Release, release, release and renew, Release, release, release and renew... Release, release, release and renew...Release...... and Renew!"

*(Stay here for a few minutes)*

You have been have lost track of time and notice the fire has gone out. The great eye on the wall of the chamber is gone now. You get up off the ground and make your way through the passageway towards what looks like an opening of the sacred cairn of Cailleach.

You wrap your shawl tighter around your shoulders as the air gets icier as you get closer to the opening.

When you arrive at the opening; you look out to see that a magnificent white mantle of snow has fallen throughout the dark moon night.

You walk out of the ancient cairn and into the morning snow. With one step in front of the other; your feet sink into and out of the snow until you come upon the ring of stones again.

You walk into the center of the ring. All is hushed and snow covered except for the great triple spiraled carved stones themselves. They hum with an ancient power. You feel lighter. You are changed. You have persevered through the dark moon night in the sacred cairn of Cailleach. Your old hurts, pains, burdens, regrets, patterns and negative stresses are gone!

You stand within the great ring of stones now with your arms held up to the sky and honor and thank wise Cailleach for her fierceness and divine gift of transformation. The triple spirals etched on the stones swirl. You spin around and dance with abandon and laughing. You are lighter, energized, charged and in harmony with all the forces of nature around you. *YOU* are part of the everlasting cycle of Life…Death…and Rebirth.

Swirling and dancing until you are once again enveloped by the thick white mist rolling off the moors and uplands.

*(pause for a minute)*

Gently take a few deep breaths. Wiggle your toes and fingers and when you are ready …Come back to present time and place. Our journey ends here.

Blessed be!

# ABOUT THE AUTHOR

*She bides by the moon...*

Bridget Engels is an Artist, Writer, Priestess, Ritualist, and
Founder of the Circle of Luna
(a women's spiritual moon circle in Seattle since 2010)

She has actively practiced the Dianic Wiccan tradition
for over 13 years and has written, planned and led private
and public women's-focused Esbat rituals and ceremonies
in the Seattle area since 2010.

She received her BFA in Painting from the
San Francisco Art Institute and has worked as an
Art Director in San Francisco, Portland and Seattle.

O    O    O

You can connect with her via Facebook on her
The Oracle of Luna page.

Made in the USA
Middletown, DE
25 June 2018